THE DESTRUCTION
OF THE UNITED STATES

THE DESTRUCTION OF THE UNITED STATES

The Key

The Destruction of the United States

Copyright © 2019 by The Key. All rights reserved.

No part of this publication may be reproduced, stored in a retrieval system or transmitted in any way by any means,
electronic, mechanical, photocopy, recording or otherwise without the prior permission of the author except as provided
by USA copyright law.

The opinions expressed by the author are not necessarily those of URLink Print and Media.

1603 Capitol Ave., Suite 310 Cheyenne, Wyoming USA 82001
1-888-980-6523 | admin@urlinkpublishing.com

URLink Print and Media is committed to excellence in the publishing industry.

Book design copyright © 2018 by URLink Print and Media. All rights reserved.
Published in the United States of America

ISBN 978-1-64367-303-5 (Paperback)
ISBN 978-1-64367-304-2 (Hardback)
ISBN 978-1-64367-302-8 (Digital)

Non-Fiction
03.05.19

FOREWORD

At a time when art books numbers are like blades of grass on an Oklahoma prairie, let it be known that all persons, courts cases, and speeches are true to the best my knowledge. Dedicated to that Indian star on that flag.

THE KEY

WAPUM KEEPER, CHEROKEES WEST

We are still riding!

INTRODUCTION

This paper is to document some of the godly principles that set up this country and made it great. Principles that were used and worked according to laws that man has not made! Like baking a cake, if you do everything right, it rises and tastes great. However, if you do not follow the recipe and do not let the dough rise, it does not work. Just as this country has departed from these godly principles, our society is being destroyed.

Protestant, a word most are familiar with made up of the words "pro" which means for and "testies" which means testify or testifying. It is used in the Latin version of *The Vulgate*, which the Roman Catholic used referring to Isaiah who was "for testifying God's word." With the degradation of language today, like the word "mother" that now can be a swear word, Protestants has a negative connotation to it as protesting against something. When the word "Protestant" was coined referring to a religious group of people. Martin Luther's followers were for testifying the errors in the church, not God's word!

HISTORY OF THE CHURCH

Thanks to the invention of the printing press, the King James translation of the Bible, and Martin Luther's discovery of old light from the word of God—which became the new light and life to that generation—they were able to read the scriptures themselves. From these people, two groups of were formed. The Separatists and the Puritans. The Separatists wanted to leave the church, so they came over to America and worshiped God the way God desires instead of the way of the Right Reverend So-and-so, the pope, or the government said they should worship God. On the other hand, the Puritans were the ones who wanted to purify the church. These were the people who came over on the

Mayflower. Talk about believing in God's hedge of protection, the boats they came over on used to haul wine. Because of the spillage, there were no rats on the boat, and they arrived disease free. Also, they had no Indian problems. The first Indian they saw, Squanto, knew how to speak English, walked into camp, and asked if they had any beer. He saw their plight and taught them how to hunt, fish, and plant corn. These are the people who endorsed these godly principles that made this country great!

This man's tribe, that used to live where the pilgrims had landed, had died from a plague, and all the other tribes thought the place was cursed and would not go there. Hence, no Indian problems. Squanto had been captured and sold into Spain as a slave, became a Christian, then sold into England. Before his master died, he was freed and given passage back to his home in America. (Acts of God)

Other side of the coin: Chief we have intruders. "Give me your thoughts." Well it is not a War Party, they have women and children. "Well let's just leave them alone and see what happens." Next year at Council, "Chief asks about the intruders, what are they doing?" Braves say, oh they are just over there starving to death. "Chief says, well let's go get Squanto."

FOUNDER'S QUOTES

The University of Houston conducted a study of the ideals of our founders. This project spanned 10 years and assembled 15,000 writings from the founding era, no small sample, that isolated 3,154 direct quotes. These quotes were from Barron Charles de Montecristo 8.3%, Sir William Blackstone 7.9%, and John Locke 2.9%. Creating no small stir, these researchers found that direct quotes from the Bible where used four times more in Montecristo, four times more in Blackstone's, and twelve times more in John Locke's. Accordingly, 34% came directly out of the Bible (Barton: 1991).

The Key

Blackstone's *Commentaries on the Laws of England* was first introduced in 1768. For the next hundred and sixty years, the law textbook of American Courts quoted Blackstone to settle disputes, to define words, and to examine procedure. These commentaries were the final words in the Supreme Court. Blackstone got his ideas from the Bible, his contemporaries also provided a biblical concept on which those laws were based. So while only 34% came directly from the Bible, 60% came from men like Blackstone who use the Bible to arrive at their own conclusions. Of those quotes, 94% came either directly or indirectly from the Bible (Barton: 1990).

A sample of some of their quotes was John Quincy Adam's speech on July 4th 1837, "Why is it that next to the birthday of the Savior of the World your most joyous and most venerated festival returns on this day the 4th of July." Why were these two the top holidays? His answer is, "Not that in the chain of human events the birthday of the nation is obviously link to the birthday of the Savior of the World, that formed the elements in the progress of the Gospel dispensation, is it not that the Declaration of Independence first organized the social compact that it laid the Cornerstone of the human government upon the first precepts of Christianity" (Newberry: Charles Whipple, 1837:5).

And the beat goes on, expressing that the biggest victory won in the American Revolution was that Christian principles and government would be tied together in what he called "indissoluble bond", but today we hear just the opposite, the separation of church and state; but that is not what he said nor what the First Amendment says. Many others spoke boldly about their Christian beliefs, like John Jay, the original Chief Justice of the US Supreme Court. One of three men most responsible for the Constitution declared, "Providence has given to our people the choice of their rulers and it is the duty as well as the privilege and interest of our Christian Nation to select and prefer Christians for their rulers" (Jay: 1789).

Do we hear the same today coming out of the Supreme Court? Nope, not at all. Was this man familiar with the original intent of the Constitution? I should say that he was. Does the father of our country have anything to offer us? Evidently, not. Why? Because his advice was to religious, stating, "Of all the depositions and habits which lead to political prosperity; religion and morality are indispensable supports. In vain would that man claimed the tribute of Patriotism who should labor to subvert these great pillars" (Richardson:1796).

Evidently, Washington believed that any man who would separate religion and morality from politics would be a traitor. These are statements of America's founders of America's history. Do we still hear this in schools? No, you might find Washington's "Farewell Address" today in schools minus the four religious remarks. Why? because it might cause brain damage. (Barton:1986).

THE COURTS

This biblical heritage was so well understood that in earlier years, the Supreme Court ruled according to the founders' intent. The US Supreme Court stated that in 1892, "our laws and our institution must necessarily be based and embody the teachings of the Redeemer of mankind. It is impossible that it should be otherwise in this sense and to this extent our civilization and our institutions are emphatically Christian" (Flood:1986). This case was not very long, only sixteen pages in the court records, but provided 187 different presidents to support its conclusion. Courts based their decisions on the presidents. Keep in mind that they had many more that they could choose from—187 was enough ! (Barton:1990).

The First Amendment never intended to separate Christian principles from government. Not very many people realize that today. The courts make rulings that opposed the rulings of the Founding Fathers made themselves. Today, all we ever hear is, "separation of church and state." These words are not even in the First Amendment. Congress shall make no law respecting the establishment of religion or prohibiting the free exercise thereof. All this means is that we do want God's principles in our government, but we do not want just one denomination running the country as it was in England.

Separation of church and state comes from a letter from President Thomas Jefferson consoling the Danbury Baptists concerning the fear of the A national/state denomination, and rightfully so, today all we hear is separation of church and state without the context or the explanation of the letter or how it was used in earlier courts. This letter was used several times by the court to keep God's principles in our systems (Barton:1990).

In 1962 however the court took a different stand using only eight words out of Jefferson's letter. The word church no longer meant, "Federal Establish

Denomination," but now it meant a, "religious activity in public." School prayer was the first victim in the 1962 Engel case remember in 1892 the court used 187 presidents. In 1962 they used ZERO presidents!

Due to this new doctrine in 1963 the courts removed Bible readings and religious classes. In the cases of Abington vs Schempp and Murry vs Curllet, the decision of the Court noted that; "If portions of the New Testament were read without explanation they could be and had been psychologically harmful to the child" (Abington vs Schempp 374 us 1963) (Murray vs Curllet at 374 us 1963).

Some proclamation to have without any historical or legal precedent. The court furthered this new man-made Doctrine in 1967 it was outlawed the posting of the Ten Commandments from hanging on the wall. Fearing that they might be obeyed! In the case of Stone vs Graham the Court noted "if the posted copies of the 10 Commandments are to have any effects at all it will be to induce the school children to read, meditate upon, perhaps to venerate and obey the Ten Commandments. This is not a permissible objective" (Stone vs Graham ; 43 us 39 (1990)).

Oh! What a wonder our courts have become. To make such a lofty decision, you cannot let these kids even see the Ten Commandments anymore because if you do, they might obey them. Things like, don't kill, don't steal, don't lie, that would be unconstitutional. Previously many presidents ruled that the school must use the bible (Vidal vs Girard`s executed ; 43 us 126, 205 – 206 1844)

When the court declares that something is unconstitutional it implies that the founders who drafted it would oppose it. James Madison Chief Architect of the Constitution is quoted saying, "we have stake the whole future of American civilization upon the power of government, far from it, we have staked the future of all of our political institutions upon the capacity of each and all of us to govern ourselves according to the Ten Commandments of God." (Barton ; 1991)

The whole episode over God and religion in the school started with the Engle vs Vitale case over a prayer that just mentioned God, "Almighty God we acknowledge our dependence upon Thee, and we beg Thy blessings upon us, our parents and our teachers, and upon our government" (Engle vs Vitale ; 370 us. 421 (1962)).

The court found out that 97% of the country did believe in God and only 3% did not. They sided with the 3%. It became the majority. Look at what the philosophy of the 3% has done to the parties of that prayer. SAT scores are down. Today, we are educating a generation who will not know as much as their parents did upon graduation. The next part of the prayer is the family. Pregnancies of unwed mothers and street crimes have shot up drastically at a 45° angle since 1962 and 63 cases. The USA is the number one of the countries in the world in divorce, violent crimes, drug abuse, voluntary abortion, and illiteracy of all the industrial nations. (Macionis:1993) Need I go on to prove Washington's warnings, "Let it be simply asked where is the security for life, for reputation, and for property if the sense of religion and obligation desert?" (Barton:1991) Certainly, we have lost our security in this country when the court rules secular humanism and atheism as religions which are practiced religiously in our schools. (Trash vs Watkins; 367 U.S. 488 (1961) (Malnak vs Yogi ; 440F. Support. 1285 (D.C. NJ. 1977)

One of George Washington's warnings in his farewell address stated, "Let us with caution indulge the supposition that morality can be maintained without religion. Whatever may be conceded to the influence of refined education of mind, reason, and experience both forbid us to expect that national morality can prevail in exclusion of religious principle." Notice the accuracy of his warning, along with every other moral measurement, the court has removed biblical teachings from the schools.

CONCLUSION

The problem in this country today is found in Hosea 4:61 "My people are destroyed for a lack of knowledge. Because they have rejected knowledge I will also reject them." God declared that His chosen people, on the inside of the pail so to speak, are destroyed for a lack of knowledge. Is this context of this scripture talking about knowledge of math, science, Playboy, or Saturday Evening Post? No, it's talking about a lack of knowledge concerning His word. When man lacks God's wisdom, he does things his own way. Let us look at the difference in Jeremiah 29:5-6 "build ye houses and dwell in them, and plant gardens and eat the fruit of them, get ye wives and have sons and daughters of them." When man does it his own way, as usual, it is ass backwards. They get somebody pregnant, decide to get married, and beat their heads up against the wall trying to buy or build a house while they are raising a family. Stupido! To be His people and reject God's word! Because they are taught that God did not write it. It is declared that the Apostle Paul wrote that it is man-made there is nothing spiritual about it at all. Jeremiah 2:13 states, "For my people have committed two evils, they have forsaken me the fountain of living water and hewed them out cisterns, furthermore, broken cisterns, that can hold no water." A fountain is an unlimited amount of knowledge that man has rejected in his schools. A cistern holds only a limited amount. Furthermore, God says that it is cracked, and when you need the supply, it won't be there. Pottery changes from culture to culture, so does their doctrines. Sometimes, it gets broken. Like a clay pot, society does not have the answers when they need it. Man on his own does not know what is wrong or how to fix it. Man cannot learn anything from within himself (Macionis:1993).

PS. The colonists did not know what liberty and freedom were until they met the Native Americans. Names of most tribes meant; "the people!" Funny, fifty strands and fifty States. Also, how they try to get prisoners to read the bible, but will do everything possible to keep it out of the classrooms and minds! That would help to keep them from going there in the first place!

The Key

Don't watch us!

The Destruction of the United States

HE sent HIS word and healed them and delivered them from their destruction.

1 Corinthians 1:27: But God hath chosen the foolish things of the world to confound the wise; and God hath chosen the weak things of the world to confound the things that are mighty.

ure 15. Hendrick, Abraham, and Franklin at the Albany Conference, 1754.

1 Corinthians 1:28: And base things of the world and things that are despised, hath God chosen, Yea, and things that are not, to bring to naught things that are.

Where do you think we got the term "let's bury the hatchet"-for make peace? Why is the top rank of a certain gang "Eagle Scout?" These terms came from the story of the Tree of Peace (the foundation of our constitution)!

Wampum strings and belts recorded their laws. The colonist did not know what freedom was until they met the Heathens!

THE KEY

They had a scheme of laws that protected the minority; all the tribes were not the same size. Their laws were like the rafters in a house; you only need so many. One set that covered all the tribes (states) and each tribe (state) could have their own. Some of our founders had some respect for our forgotten founders. The thirteen arrows in this seal, recall the suggestion of Canassatego (treaty conference of 1775) to unite as they had done five hundred years earlier! The model of the laws of this country was not and is not an experiment. A certain tribe sent a soul to England before the Revolutionary War and came back to his tribe after the war with a Bible in his hand and said, "This is a very good book; but they are not very good students!" What a shame we only accepted so little of their wisdom!

Figure 32. In 1775, treaty commissioners at Albany recall the words of Canassatego. By John Kahionhes Fadden.

The Destruction of the United States

Mighty Hunter   Never do it again

Probably going to get his legs scratched
(twigged) for bowering the rifle. (:-)))

The Key

Light Horsemen

Never Get Away

What they called the police of Indian Territory.
The Natives knew how to take their own medicine.

The Destruction of the United States

These Light Horseman are doing this to their own people. Not a racial matter, just a correction activity. The reason why they did not have a prison economy was that the people knew how to take their own medicine. Warrior's brother was to be "twigged" but the brother fainted. The Warrior cut him loose and said, "Give them to me, we do raise some men in our family."

THE KEY

The second time, they double the twinging, but the third time they would just go ahead and shoot them for being untrainable. Circle of life: the Natives believed in God with more sincerity than the Colonists. The Native Americans believed in God, the Supreme Creator of the universe and the above beings.

Fore similarities between the US Constitution and the American Native's way of peace–"Checks and Balances " see, "The Confederacy of the Six Nations" by Ely Parker and Lewis Henry Morgan.

"Liberty Exemplar" by Donald Grindle and Bruce Johansen, which can be read online.

"Sharper Axes, Lower Taxes" by Phillip Booth. An IEA report for the UN that they funded and can be read online.

Civilization—not very good. Students will not even follow their own advice! Stupido!

Quote from Benjamin Franklin says, "It would be a very strange thing if a group of ignorant savages should be capable of forming a scheme for such a Union… and yet for a like Union should be impractical for ten or a dozen colonies, to whom it is more necessary."

THE KEY

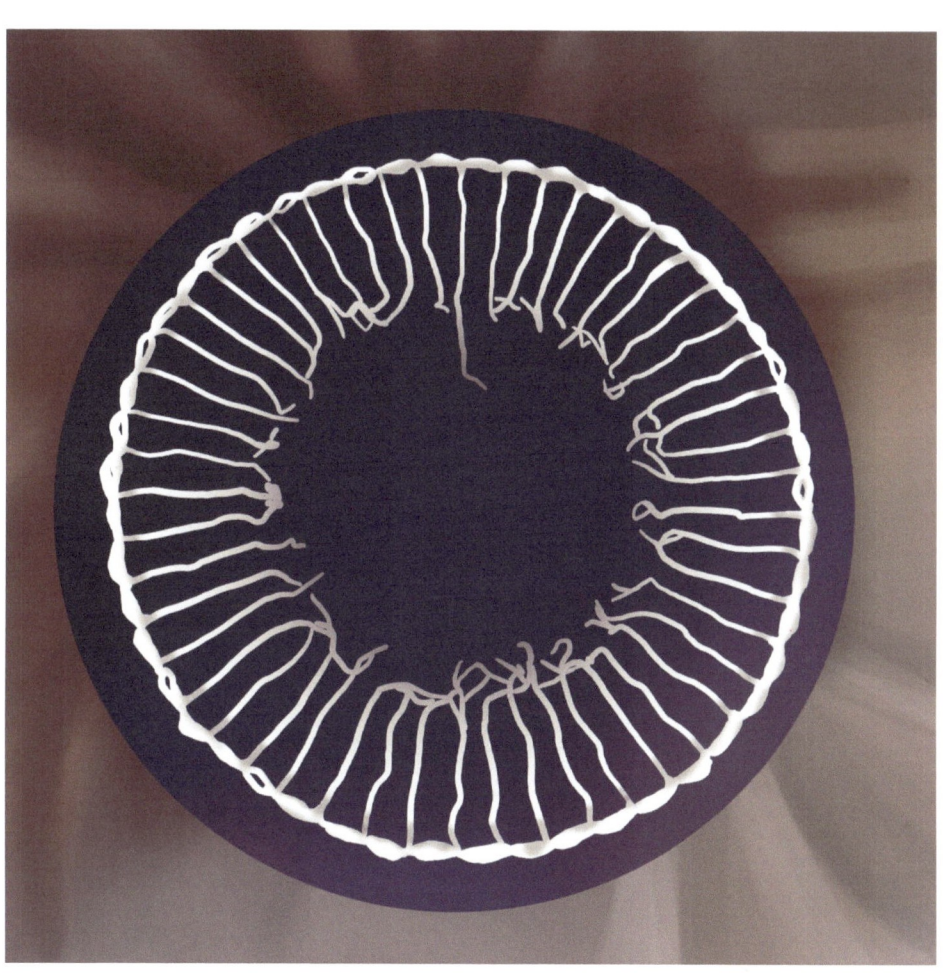

The checks and balances in this String of Wampum Beads are the foundation of our constitution, our once Republic.

OTHER THINGS AND MATTERS

In 1928, the U.S. Training Manual (used for all men in service uniform) gave to them a quite accurate definition of a democracy: "A government of the masses. Authority derived through mass meetings or any form of 'direct' expression. Results in MOBOCRACY. Attitude toward law that the will of the majority shall regulate, whether it be based upon deliberation or governed by passion, prejudice, and impulse, without restraint or regard to consequences. Results in demagogism, license, agitation, discontent, anarchy!" That was in 1928. Just when that true explanation was dropped and through what intermediate changes the definition went, I have not had sufficient time and opportunity to learn, but compare that 1928 statement with what is said in the same place and for the same sense by 1952 in the "Soldiers Guide," Department of the Army Field Manual issued in 1952, we find the following meaning of democracy. Because the United States is a democracy, the majority of the people decide how our government will be organized and run, and that includes the Army, the Navy, and the Air Force. The people do this by electing representatives, and these men and women then carry out the wishes of the people. (Just not very good students) Geez, have they ever said the "Pledge of allegiance" or fought in wars overseas to spread Republicanism? Geez!

Ely Parker a Seneca Shekem: representative of the tribe. He was educated in engineering, was working on a channel, Erie Canal and some lighthouses, on the right end of a shovel. He was the boss or advisor. He had two hobbies, getting drunk and fighting. Well, Ulessey S. Grant I think lived in Gallina, and the two of them got to be really good friends (like to do the same thing.) Well, after the Civil War started, Grant got Parker to be his aid-de-camp. After Grant was elected president, he sent Parker on a mission to collect all the checks and balances of all the old chiefs he could find to record what was left of the checks and balances of their old ways, thus, "The Confederacy of the Six Nations." He found French papers doing the same in Canada with a little Jesuit input.

THE KEY

Half-breed born in "No man's Land" Indian Territory. Half
from Texas & half from Oklahoma both with Chickamuaga ancestors-Cherokee Stock that did not want to be CIVILIZED! Seen the war between the haves and have-nots in Europe. Is that not what they are trying to get us to fight over now? And wanted no part of it! Started migrating in the 1700's. To the Washita River and grants given by Spain to my father's side of family (and tribe), got along just fine with the Comanches, chased different resources traded every year. Three major migrations to Ghost town of Cherokee Town in

OK. Two from Texas and one from Civil War, too close to the Comanches, neither army wanted to go there. My grandfather moved the family to Norman OK in a covered wagon from Texas because of racism. Oklahoma is a home of the red man. Father was a bombardier in WWII, there was a time that if you worked for the Air Force, my mother's name was on the bottom of your check. One of five siblings, #4, three brothers (all dead) were cadets and vets, sister was an engineer on B-1As. Raised as a white man, before school and after spent a lot of time at Chickasaw lady's feet. Times I know of my Heavenly Father pinching His fingers keeping me alive, mother unable to nurse me, 6 or 7, leg caught in between blades on a disc,(out of house) scull crushed about the size of a cue ball, beaten and battered and left for dead, twice. 1 st one I probably deserved, 2 nd time, they thought I was somebody else. Two Ginny-pig heart ops. Total of 17 hrs under. But the best part of my life is the fact that I had a GIFTED TEACHER teach me how to rightly divide God's word. II Timothy 2:15

The Key

IMPEACHMENT AND HIGH CRIMES & MISDEMEANORS

Which of these is a "high crime:" murder, rape, or stealing a loaf of bread? These are crimes, but only high crimes if done by persons who took an oath such as insulting the Commander in Chief. That is not a crime for an ordinary, but if you were a general, it is a conduct unbecoming an officer because of the oath he took. The higher the office the higher the crime. In the old forgotten and unknown days, if a Chief picked his nose or scratched his ass in public, or anything that embarrassed his people, they could jerk him out of office. Well, this Obummer fellow has showed his ass to the world, which has embarassed me, and I do not think he can open his mouth without lying, and if you want to talk in about indisputable facts, he signed an executive order about not spending any money on abortions to buy some votes for his health care plan.

THE KEY

Call it lying or breaking a promise, definitely not a conduct becoming of the president of the United States. He took an oath too. It has been a while since I read it, but I do not think that those actions are in his handbook and are impeachable offenses. (Http:www.constiution.org/cmt/Highcrimes.htm)

It would be a very strange thing if the Six Nations of ignorant savages should be capable of forming a scheme for such a union and be able to execute it in such a manner as that it has subsidized for ages and appears indissoluble, and yet, a like union should be impractical for 10 or dozen English colonies. A quote from Benjamin Franklin.

Saw General Patraus on TV, talking about some of the things he was dealing with. Tribes squabbling with the Taliban, their own government, us, each other, and about how to survive. So, have patience and I will tell you the short version or what I can remember about the story of the Tree of Peace—the foundation of our Constitution!

There were five tribes fussing and fighting all the time for five generations, and one very evil man who had control or scared many people. There was also a man, Dekanawidah. Let's call him D, the Peacemaker. D thought and thought about how to stop the fighting and God showed him a plan that would work. D could not speak very well, so he got Hiawatha to speak for him. They we're able to travel from tribe to tribe because of the help they received from the women who were tired of losing their husbands, sons, and grandsons in battle. The first woman who fed him told him that his plan would succeed.

After they convinced all the tribes, the tribes told D and Hiawatha about this very evil man, so they went to this camp and healed him and told him of their plan to uproot this pine tree and bury all the weapons of war, and then replant it so all the people, the five tribes that agreed on the wisdom of the laws, could seek shelter from its boughs. They told the man that they had healed that he could even be the leader because of all of the checks and balances after they had replanted the tree, the white spiritually pure white roots of peace would reach to the four corners of the world. Remember, the only reason they had these laws was because they saw the evil that gets into a man's heart when he gets into a position of power. By the way, they opened their meetings with a prayer to the Supreme Creator of the universe, the Great Spirit, and you could not be a representative unless you believe in him and expected to be judged by him at your death!

Please check this site on what happened on our 200th birthday. http://www.kahonwes.com/Iroquois /document1.html

We need to reteach ourselves and try to plant some Peace Trees in Iraq and Afghanistan to stop all this squabbling and death.

Proverbs 6:4 states. "The Lord has made all things for Himself; yea even the wicked for the day of evil."

Thomas Jefferson described the Declaration of Independence as an "expression of the Native American mind."

Washington and others were trying to get the Native Americans to help in fighting the Revolutionary War. So, some Mohawks went over to England to find out who they were getting in bed with and came back so disgusted because of the haves and the have-nots. They said, "Seeing as you are already fighting on our land we will help you out, but we do not want to be any part of you. We want our own state and our own laws." See first treaty by the Continental Congress and the Delaware Valley. So you should see that the founders of this country were just learning about freedom and liberty, something the Native Americans had enjoyed for over 500 years, so say the wampum beads at the Smithsonian Museum. The founders of this country did not even know what freedom and liberty was until they met the Americans! And you should know that the spirit that worketh now in the children of disobedience is doing the same thing to the Americans of today that they did to the Americans of yesterday—take away their land and laws and rights and in the end their children. Today, you can see in UN Agenda 21; in the end, their children, boarding schools the "race to the top", and "no child left behind." See any similarities here?

I am from Oklahoma. Also, have work in nine different states. I was a carpenter New York, New Jersey, and California. I was a rough neck in Colorado, Texas, Utah, Wyoming, and Louisiana. The reputation of my forerunners left us a good reputation (you were an Okie, you went to front of the line). A person is not only willing to work (the unions up north able to sit on their ass) but able to work and get things done (bit turning to the right making new hole). I was proud I was able and willing to do the same. I mean, we stood out. I do not believe that the next generation of Okies will be like that because of the national standard grant money teaching to the test. They will be nothing but a standard of mediocrity. Our big-eared friend in the White House said he would try anything (another lie). Well, the Cherokee Tribe had more college graduates when the state of Sequoyah was denied than in the state of Texas and Arkansas put together and fluent in two languages. Now, in the state of the home of the Redman, you want to follow the lead of these "civilized people?"

I have forgotten more scriptures than most people have ever known and do not enjoy being called a Christian. Dunked, dripped, and dry-cleaned, all reading same book, sort of same book. Most people search the Scripture to collaborate what they already believe, few searched the Word of God to learn anything.

May their rivers of understanding flow together, and you God, heal this age with the mystery of your gospel of grace.

The Destruction of the United States

THE KEY

"Through the tender mercies of GOD; whereby the dayspring from on High hath visited us, to give light to them that sit in darkness and in the shadow of death, guide our feet into the way of PEACE."

Roosters crow and hens cackle. So, you are in a good place to make an impact. Hit something hard enough to be heard. The Greek word *tupos* is where we get the word for "type." Clicking-click, tappity-tap—to sound out!

"For the Word of God is quick and powerful and sharper than any two-edge sword, piercing even to the dividing asunder of soul and spirit, and of the joints and marrow, and is a discerner of the thoughts and intents of the Heart."

The number of times a word is used in scripture has a purpose. For example, there is a certain word translated as "strength". This word is used twice. First was when God cursed Cain, and said, "He was going to take the strength of the ground away from him" (Gen. 4:12). Cain was a farmer and knew what that meant and nearly killed himself over it! The second time was when it was used to talk about Samson's strength. So we know we are dealing with spiritual strengths: things and matters.

The verse above has the most words that are only used one time in all of the Scripture! Let's throw in verse 13 of Hebrews chapter 4, and we can see some of the structure of God's Word that you will find in no other writings of men.

Reason: God's Word—this is the structure of these verses.

    A. God whose Word is wonderful.
    B. What His Word is: quick = lively, powerful, and sharp.
    C. What His Word does: pierces and dividing asunder.
    B. What His Word is: a critic of the heart.
    A. God whose eye sees all.

Sharper, piercing, joints, marrow, and **discerner** (Greek word *kritikos*) are only found in this verse. To discern the thoughts and intents of the heart. What English word do you think came from the word *kritikos*? **CRITIC.**

The written word is a sword (Ephesians 6:17).

The **living** Word has a sword (Revelations 1:16 Also 19:15).

Once and only once did **God** use the word **kritikos** confining it to His own word "critic". That word is to be our judge (John 12:48), however, the powers-that-be claim that word and dare to sit in judgment of that very same word, which is to judge them. In what they term as **"higher criticism"**, which is only human reasoning based on the deceits of their own hearts. Today is man's day, he does the judging, **but** there is going to be a day and that day will be called **The Lord's Day,** and we are not talking about Sunday!

But in that **day C.J.** will have a can of whoop-ass in His back pocket and some rewards to hand out. And man will be criticized, judged by the very same word he now sits in judgment of, dividing asunder of spiritual matters and spiritual things.

They still have not put life underneath a microscope nor can doctors tell where the bone and marrow starts or stops.

So, after a while, if you want to, you might request the **governors** and the **school superintendents** and other **"public servants"** to put back into the classroom "The New England Primer" published in 1777 by the Congress for learning the ABCs for reading and writing (worked for over 150 years) Also, the Supreme Court is out of bounds prohibiting its use (Not in their handbook to pass laws!). Oklahoma should be the first state to take this challenge and use Andrew Jackson's own excuse for when they took our lands away and say, **"Let them enforce it. "**

    For believers (of anything) know this, the <u>criticizer</u>, will divide the difference between soul and spirit in that day and differentiate between that which is begotten of flesh and that which is begotten of spirit, in the individual and in the natural man.

    Don't forget the "higher powers" try to get prisoners to read the Bible yet will do all things possible to keep it out of the classrooms or children's minds that would help from getting them there in the first place.

Worth a moment, what is the meaning of "Laus Deo."

One detail that is seldom mentioned, is that in Washington, DC, there can never be a building of greater height than the Washington Monument.

With all the uproar about the removing of the Ten Commandments, etc., this is worth a moment or two of your time.

I was not aware of this amazing historical information. On the aluminum cap atop the Washington Monument in Washington, DC, are displayed two words: Laus Deo. No one can see these words. In fact, most visitors to the monument are totally unaware that they are even there, and for that matter, probably couldn't care less.

Once you know history of "Laus Deo" you will want to share this with everyone you know. These words has been there for many years. They are 550 feet and 5.125 inches high perched atop the monument, facing skyward to the father of our nation, and overlooking the 69 square miles which compromise the District of Columbia, capital of the United States of America.

Laus Deo! Two seemingly insignificant words.

The Key

Out of sight and, one might think, out of mind but very meaningfully placed at the highest point over what is the most powerful city in the most successful nation in the world.

So, what do these two words in Latin composed of just four syllables and only seven letters mean?

Very simply, they say, "**Praise be to God!**"

Though construction of this giant obelisk began in 1848, when James Polk was president of the United States, it was not until 1888 that the monument was inaugurated and open to the public.

It took twenty-five years to finally cap the memorial with a tribute to the **Father** of our nation, "**Laus Deo**", Praise be to God.

From the top this magnificent granite marble structure visitors may take in the beautiful panoramic view of the city with this division into four major segments. From that vantage point, one can also easily see the original plan of the designer, " Pierre Charles L'Enfant. A perfect cross imposed upon the landscape with the White House to the north, the Jefferson Memorial to the south, the Capitol to the east, and the Lincoln Memorial to the west.

A cross, you ask? Why a cross?

What about separation of church and state?

Yes, a cross, separation of church and state was **NOT, is NOT,** in the Constitution.

How interesting, and no doubt, intended to carry a profound meaning for those who bother to notice.

When the cornerstone of the Washington Monument was laid on July 4th, 1848, deposited with it were many items including the Holy Bible presented by the Bible Society. Praise be to God! Such was the discipline, the moral direction, and the spiritual mood given by the founder and first President of our unique Republic—one nation under God.

I am awed by George Washington's prayer for America. Have you ever read it? Well, now is your unique opportunity, so read on.

> Almighty God; We make our earnest prayer that THOU wilt keep the United States In Thy holy protection; that Thou wilt incline the hearts of the citizens to cultivate a spirit of subordination and obedience to government; and entertain a brotherly affection and love for one another and their fellow citizens of the United States at large. And finally that Thou wilt most graciously be pleased to dispose us all to do justice, to love **MERCY,** and to demean

ourselves with that charity, humility, and pacific temper of mind which were the characteristics of the Devine Author of our blessed religion, and without a humble imitation of whose example in these things we can never hope to be a happy nation. Grant our supplication, we beseech Thee, through Jesus Christ our Lord. AMEN.

Laus Deo!

I hope you will send this to every sister, brother, mother, or friend. And that they will not find it offensive, because you have given them a lesson in history that they probably never learned in school. With that, be not ashamed, or afraid, but have pity on those who will never see this because someone failed to send it on.

Thank you, Charlie and Charley,
for sending it to me.
Author unknown

THE DESTRUCTION OF THE UNITED STATES

Most ancient star maps (4 of them 4,000 years old.) Has a Sphinx with the head of a woman in-between the constellations of Leo and Virgo. Telling you where to open the book THE MOST HIGH put in the heaven, revealing the story of HIS son. Born of a woman coming back as the Lion of the Tribe of Judah. Look at Hercules foot being on top of the constellation of Drako the Dragon is equal to Gennies 3:15 that he would bruise his heel upon its head. Heaven is choke full of prophecy about C.J. and HIS fame.

See you here, there, or in the air,
The Key.
1 Thessalonians 4:16 through 1 Thessalonians 5: 11

Pay attention to the pronouns [we and they] and [us and them] and the timing of events.
GOD BLESS

www.ingramcontent.com/pod-product-compliance
Ingram Content Group UK Ltd.
Pitfield, Milton Keynes, MK11 3LW, UK
UKHW061402260426
12048UKWH00054B/2